THE
ESSENTIAL
ETHERIDGE
KNIGHT

THE ESSENTIAL
ETHERIDGE KNIGHT

ETHERIDGE KNIGHT

University of Pittsburgh Press

Published by the University of Pittsburgh Press, Pittsburgh, Pa. 15260
Copyright © 1986, Etheridge Knight
Manufactured in the United States of America
Printed on acid-free paper
10 9

Library of Congress Cataloging-in-Publication Data
Knight, Etheridge.
    The essential Etheridge Knight

    (Pitt poetry series)
    I. Title. II. Series.
    PS3561.N45A6   1986   811'.54   86-6989
    ISBN 0-8229-3529-5
    ISBN 0-8229-5378-1 (pbk.)

Most of these poems have been previously published under the title *Born of a Woman* (Houghton Mifflin, 1980), and others have appeared in *Poetry East, The American Poetry Review, Hanging Loose, The Mickle Street Review,* and *The Painted Bride Quarterly.* "Circling the Daughter" was first published as a broadside by Slash and Burn Press, Philadelphia.

I thank and acknowledge my editor, Ed Ochester, for his ideas and guidance; I thank Lynne Walker, and the poets of the Toledo Poetry Center for support and encouragement; I thank Deta (Salome) Galloway, whose love and support was, and is, a Delight and a Dilemma; thanks to Doug Margolis for typing and suggesting, and for fighting the racism in South Africa; thanks to the Reverend Gerald Cunningham, a Fellow Traveler, for supporting me in too many ways to list; and finally, my thanks—all praises due—to Elizabeth Gordon McKim for the Light of her Love, and for her tidal toleration.

The publication of this book is supported by grants from the National Endowment for the Arts in Washington, D.C., a Federal agency, and the Pennsylvania Council on the Arts.

Dedicated to my family

my mother, Mrs. Belzora Knight Taylor;
my brother, Sgt. Floyd Knight (U.S. Army, retired);
my sisters, Clyneese Knight Bennett, Eunice Knight
Bowens, and Janice Juanita Knight

And to the memory of

my father, BuShie; my brother, Charles;
and my sister, Lois Ivy Knight

CONTENTS

CONTENTS

CONTENTS

CONTENTS

THE
ESSENTIAL
ETHERIDGE
KNIGHT

GENESIS

the skin
of my poems
May be green, yes,
and sometimes
wrinkled
or worn

the snake shape
of my song
may cause
the heel
of Adam & Eve
to bleed . . .

split my skin
with the rock
of love old
as the rock
of Moses
my poems
love you

1

HARD ROCK RETURNS TO PRISON
FROM THE HOSPITAL
FOR THE CRIMINAL INSANE

Hard Rock / was / "known not to take no shit
From nobody," and he had the scars to prove it:
Split purple lips, lumbed ears, welts above
His yellow eyes, and one long scar that cut
Across his temple and plowed through a thick
Canopy of kinky hair.

The WORD / was / that Hard Rock wasn't a mean nigger
Anymore, that the doctors had bored a hole in his head,
Cut out part of his brain, and shot electricity
Through the rest. When they brought Hard Rock back,
Handcuffed and chained, he was turned loose,
Like a freshly gelded stallion, to try his new status.
And we all waited and watched, like a herd of sheep,
To see if the WORD was true.

As we waited we wrapped ourselves in the cloak
Of his exploits: "Man, the last time, it took eight
Screws to put him in the Hole." "Yeah, remember when he
Smacked the captain with his dinner tray?" "He set
The record for time in the Hole—67 straight days!"
"Ol Hard Rock! man, that's one crazy nigger."
And then the jewel of a myth that Hard Rock had once bit
A screw on the thumb and poisoned him with syphilitic spit.

The testing came, to see if Hard Rock was really tame.
A hillbilly called him a black son of a bitch
And didn't lose his teeth, a screw who knew Hard Rock
From before shook him down and barked in his face.
And Hard Rock did *nothing*. Just grinned and looked silly,
His eyes empty like knot holes in a fence.

7

And even after we discovered that it took Hard Rock
Exactly 3 minutes to tell you his first name,
We told ourselves that he had just wised up,
Was being cool; but we could not fool ourselves for long,
And we turned away, our eyes on the ground. Crushed.
He had been our Destroyer, the doer of things
We dreamed of doing but could not bring ourselves to do,
The fears of years, like a biting whip,
Had cut deep bloody grooves
Across our backs.

CELL SONG

Night   Music   Slanted
Light strike the cave
of sleep. I alone
tread the red circle
and twist the space
with speech.

Come now, etheridge, don't
be a savior; take
your words and scrape
the sky, shake rain

on the desert, sprinkle
salt on the tail
of a girl,

can there anything
good come out of
prison

HE SEES THROUGH STONE

He sees through stone
he has the secret eyes
this old black one
who under prison skies
sits pressed by the sun
against the western wall
his pipe between purple gums

the years fall
like overripe plums
bursting red flesh
on the dark earth

his time is not my time
but I have known him
in a time gone

he led me trembling cold
into the dark forest
taught me the secret rites
to make it with a woman
to be true to my brothers
to make my spear drink
the blood of my enemies

now black cats circle him
flash white teeth
snarl at the air
mashing green grass beneath
shining muscles

ears peeling his words
he smiles
he knows
the hunt   the enemy
he has the secret eyes
he sees through stone

THE IDEA OF ANCESTRY

1

Taped to the wall of my cell are 47 pictures: 47 black
faces: my father, mother, grandmothers (1 dead), grand-
fathers (both dead), brothers, sisters, uncles, aunts,
cousins (1st & 2nd), nieces, and nephews. They stare
across the space at me sprawling on my bunk. I know
their dark eyes, they know mine. I know their style,
they know mine. I am all of them, they are all of me;
they are farmers, I am a thief, I am me, they are thee.

I have at one time or another been in love with my mother,
1 grandmother, 2 sisters, 2 aunts (1 went to the asylum),
and 5 cousins. I am now in love with a 7-yr-old niece
(she sends me letters written in large block print, and
her picture is the only one that smiles at me).

I have the same name as 1 grandfather, 3 cousins, 3 nephews,
and 1 uncle. The uncle disappeared when he was 15, just took
off and caught a freight (they say). He's discussed each year
when the family has a reunion, he causes uneasiness in
the clan, he is an empty space. My father's mother, who is 93
and who keeps the Family Bible with everybody's birth dates
(and death dates) in it, always mentions him. There is no
place in her Bible for "whereabouts unknown."

2

Each fall the graves of my grandfathers call me, the brown
hills and red gullies of mississippi send out their electric
messages, galvanizing my genes. Last yr / like a salmon quitting
the cold ocean-leaping and bucking up his birthstream / I

hitchhiked my way from LA with 16 caps in my pocket and a
monkey on my back. And I almost kicked it with the kinfolks.
I walked barefooted in my grandmother's backyard / I smelled the
  old
land and the woods / I sipped cornwhiskey from fruit jars with the
  men /
I flirted with the women / I had a ball till the caps ran out
and my habit came down. That night I looked at my grandmother
and split / my guts were screaming for junk / but I was almost
contented / I had almost caught up with me.
(The next day in Memphis I cracked a croaker's crib for a fix.)

This yr there is a gray stone wall damming my stream, and when
the falling leaves stir my genes, I pace my cell or flop on my bunk
and stare at 47 black faces across the space. I am all of them,
they are all of me, I am me, they are thee, and I have no children
to float in the space between.

ON THE YARD

A slim
young fascist
fresh from the Hole
slid into me
murdered me
with his eyes
and said, "Man,
why ain't you
doing something?"

All night
I sat up
All night
wrote 5,000 words
explaining how
I
was doing something

but the slim cat—
beautiful fascist
didn't buy
it—nor
did I
completely.

A WASP WOMAN VISITS
A BLACK JUNKIE IN PRISON

After explanations and regulations, he
Walked warily in.
Black hair covered his chin, subscribing to
Villainous ideal.
"This can not be real," he thought, "this is a
Classical mistake;
This is a cake baked with embarrassing icing;
Somebody's got
Likely as not, a big fat tongue in cheek!
What have I to do
With a prim and proper-blooded lady?"
Christ in deed has risen
When a Junkie in prison visits with a Wasp woman.

"Hold your stupid face, man,
Learn a little grace, man; drop a notch the sacred shield.
She might have good reason,
Like: 'I was in prison and ye visited me not,' or—some such.
So sweep clear
Anachronistic fear, fight the fog,
And use no hot words."

After the seating
And the greeting, they fished for a denominator,
Common or uncommon;
And could only summon up the fact that both were human.
"Be at ease, man!
Try to please, man!—the lady is as lost as you:
'You got children, Ma'am?' " he said aloud.

The thrust broke the dam, and their lines wiggled in the water.
She offered no pills
To cure his many ills, no compact sermons, but small
And funny talk:
"My baby began to walk . . . simply cannot keep his room
    clean . . ."
Her chatter sparked no resurrection and truly
No shackles were shaken
But after she had taken her leave, he walked softly,
And for hours used no hot words.

HAIKU

1

Eastern guard tower
glints in sunset; convicts rest
like lizards on rocks.

2

The piano man
is stingy at 3 A.M.
his songs drop like plum.

3

Morning sun slants cell.
Drunks stagger like cripple flies
On jailhouse floor.

4

To write a blues song
is to regiment riots
and pluck gems from graves.

5

A bare pecan tree
slips a pencil shadow down
a moonlit snow slope.

6

The falling snow flakes
Cannot blunt the hard aches nor
Match the steel stillness.

7

Under moon shadows
A tall boy flashes knife and
Slices star bright ice.

8

In the August grass
Struck by the last rays of sun
The cracked teacup screams.

9

Making jazz swing in
Seventeen syllables AIN'T
No square poet's job.

FOR FRECKLE-FACED GERALD

Now you take ol Rufus. He beat drums,
was free and funky under the arms,
fucked white girls, jumped off a bridge
(and thought nothing of the sacrilege),
he copped out—and he was over twenty-one.

Take Gerald. Sixteen years hadn't even done
a good job on his voice. He didn't even know
how to talk tough, or how to hide the glow
of life before he was thrown in as "pigmeat"
for the buzzards to eat.

Gerald, who had no memory or hope of copper hot lips—
of firm upthrusting thighs
to reinforce his flow,
let tall walls and buzzards change the course
of his river from south to north.

(No safety in numbers, like back on the block:
two's aplenty. three? definitely not.
four? "you're all muslims."
five? "you were planning a race riot."
plus, Gerald could never quite win
with his precise speech and innocent grin
the trust and fists of the young black cats.)

Gerald, sun-kissed ten thousand times on the nose
and cheeks, didn't stand a chance,
didn't even know that the loss of his balls
had been plotted years in advance
by wiser and bigger buzzards than those
who now hover above his track
and at night light upon his back.

THE WARDEN SAID TO ME
THE OTHER DAY

The warden said to me the other day
(innocently, I think), "Say, etheridge,
why come the black boys don't run off
like the white boys do?"
I lowered my jaw and scratched my head
and said (innocently, I think), "Well, suh,
I ain't for sure, but I reckon it's 'cause
we ain't got nowheres to run to."

MY LIFE, THE QUALITY OF WHICH

My life, the quality of which
From the moment
My Father grunted and comed
Until now
As the sounds of my words
Bruise your ears
IS
and can be felt
In the one word: DESPERATION

But you have to *feel* for it

Jefferson, Missouri
June 9, 1972

A POEM FOR BLACK RELOCATION CENTERS

Flukum couldn't stand the strain. Flukum
wanted inner and outer order, so
he joined the army where U.S. Manuals made
everything plain—even how to button his shirt,
and how to kill yellow men. (If Flukum
ever felt hurt or doubt about who his enemy
was, the Troop Information Officer or the Stars
and Stripes straightened him out.)
And, we must not forget
that Flukum was paid well to let the Red
Blood. And sin? If Flukum ever thought about sin
or Hell for squashing the yellow men, the good Chaplain
(Holy by God and by Congress) pointed out with
Devilish skill that to kill the colored men was not
altogether a sin.

Flukum marched back from the war, straight and tall,
and with presents for all: a water pipe for daddy,
teeny teacups for mama, sheer silk for tittee, and
a jade inlaid dagger for me. But, with a smile
on his face in a place just across the bay,
Flukum, the patriot, got shot that same day,
got shot in his great wide chest, bedecked with good
conduct ribbons. He died surprised, he had thought
the enemy far away on the other side of the sea.

YOU ARE

—for E. C. A.

You are a Sunrise
And a bright Star
And the Light that Lingers
in the middle of my Lake.

THE VIOLENT SPACE
(or when your sister sleeps around for money)

Exchange in greed the ungraceful signs. Thrust
The thick notes between green apple breasts.
Then the shadow of the devil descends,
The violent space cries and angel eyes,
Large and dark, retreat in innocence and in ice.
(Run sister run—the Bugga man comes!)

The violent space cries silently,
Like you cried wide years ago
In another space, speckled by the sun
And the leaves of a green plum tree,
And you were stung
By a red wasp and we flew home.
(Run sister run—the Bugga man comes!)

Well, hell, lil sis, wasps still sting.
You are all of seventeen and as alone now
In your pain as you were with the sting
On your brow.
Well, shit, lil sis, here we are:
You and I and this poem.
And what should I do? should I squat
In the dust and make strange markings on the ground?
Shall I chant a spell to drive the demon away?
(Run sister run—the Bugga man comes!)

In the beginning you were the Virgin Mary,
And you are the Virgin Mary now.
But somewhere between Nazareth and Bethlehem
You lost your name in the nameless void.
"O Mary don't you weep don't you moan"
O Mary shake your butt to the violent juke,
Absorb the demon puke and watch the white eyes pop,
(Run sister run—the Bugga man comes!)

And what do I do. I boil my tears in a twisted spoon
And dance like an angel on the point of a needle.
I sit counting syllables like Midas gold.
I am not bold. I cannot yet take hold of the demon
And lift his weight from you black belly,
So I grab the air and sing my song.
(But the air cannot stand my singing long.)

A POEM FOR A CERTAIN LADY
ON HER 33rd BIRTHDAY

Who are we, S. S.,
to ride the curves of air
or to worry about the waning moon?
The mountains will not tremble
and the sea will not give up her dead.

Time is now, said the African Poet.
Unfelt as our touch
across these seasons
unending as the circle
of our dead fathers and unborn sons—
the rise and fall of our laughter—
the measure of our steps
as we move to each other.

Years are the strips of tinsel
hanging on hunky brains
Our time is the constant blooming
of our love.

THE STRETCHING OF THE BELLY

—for Charlene Blackburn

Marks / of the mother are
Your / self
Stretching
Reaching
For life
For love

Markings are / not to / be mocked
Markings are medicants
Markings / are / signs
Along the hi / way

Scars are / not
Marking scars do / not / come from stars
Or the moon Scars come from wars
From war / men who plunge
Like a bayonet into the gut
Or like a blackjack against the skull
Or prick
Like the end of a safety pin

Scars are stripes of slavery
Like my back
Not your belly
Which / is bright
And bringing forth
Making / music

AS YOU LEAVE ME

Shiny record albums scattered over
the living room floor, reflecting light
from the lamp, sharp reflections that hurt
my eyes as I watch you, squatting among the platters,
the beer foam making mustaches on your lips.

And, too,
the shadows on your cheeks from your long lashes
fascinate me—almost as much as the dimples
in your cheeks, your arms, and your legs.

You
hum along with Mathis—how you love Mathis!
with his burnished hair and quicksilver voice that dances
among the stars and whirls through canyons
like windblown snow, sometimes I think that Mathis
could take you from me if you could be complete
without me. I glance at my watch. It is now time.

You rise,
silently, and to the bedroom and the paint;
on the lips red, on the eyes black,
and I lean in the doorway and smoke, and see you
grow old before my eyes, and smoke. why do you
chatter while you dress? and smile when you grab
your large leather purse? don't you know that when you
leave me I walk to the window and watch you? and light
a reefer as I watch you? and I die as I watch you
disappear in the dark streets
to whistle and smile at the johns.

NO MOON FLOODS THE MEMORY
OF THAT NIGHT

No moon floods the memory of that night
only the rain I remember the cold rain
against our faces and mixing with your tears
only the rain I remember the cold rain
and your mouth soft and warm
no moon no stars no jagged pain
of lightning only my impotent tongue
and the red rage within my brain
knowing that the chilling rain was our forever
even as I tried to explain:

"A revolutionary is a doomed man
with no certainties but love and history."
"But our children must grow up with certainties
and they will make the revolution."
"By example we must show the way so plain
that our children can go neither right
nor left but straight to freedom."
"No," you said. And you left.

No moon floods the memory of that night
only the rain I remember the cold rain
and praying that like the rain
returns to the sky you would return to me again.

UPON YOUR LEAVING

—for Sonia

Night
and in the warm blackness
your woman smell filled the room
and our rivers flowed together. became one
my love's patterns. our sweat / drenched bellies
made flat cracks as we kissed
like sea waves lapping against the shore
rocks rising and rolling and sliding back.

And
your sighs softly calling my name
became love songs child / woman songs
old as a thousand years new as the few
smiles you released like sacred doves. and I
fell asleep, ashamed of my glow of my halo, and
ignoring them who waited below
to take you away when the sun rose . . .

Day
and the sunlight playing in the green leaves
above us fell across your face traced the tears
in your eyes and love patterns in the wet grass.
and as they waited inside in triumphant patience
to take you away I begged you to stay.
"but, etheridge," you said, "i don't know what to do."
and the love patterns shifted and shimmered in your eyes.

And
after they had taken you and gone, the day
turned stark white. bleak. barren like
the nordic landscape. I turned and entered

into the empty house and fell on the floor
laughing. trying to fill the spaces your love had left.
knowing that we would not remain apart long.
our rivers had flowed together.
we are one.
and are strong.

FEELING FUCKED UP

Lord she's gone done left me done packed / up and split
and I with no way to make her
come back and everywhere the world is bare
bright bone white   crystal sand glistens
dope death dead dying and jiving drove
her away made her take her laughter and her smiles
and her softness and her midnight sighs—

Fuck Coltrane and music and clouds drifting in the sky
fuck the sea and trees and the sky and birds
and alligators and all the animals that roam the earth
fuck marx and mao fuck fidel and nkrumah and
democracy and communism fuck smack and pot
and red ripe tomatoes fuck joseph fuck mary fuck
god jesus and all the disciples fuck fanon nixon
and malcolm fuck the revolution fuck freedom fuck
the whole muthafucking thing
all i want now is my woman back
so my soul can sing

Vigo County

Beyond the brown hill
Above the silent cedars,
Blackbirds flee April rains.

The Penal Farm

The wire fence is tall.
The lights in the prison barracks
Flick off, one by one.

Crown Hill Cemetery, Indianapolis

A black and white dog
Sniffs gravestone to gravestone:
Pees on Hoosier Poet.

Indianapolis War Memorial

Young boys play in pairs,
Touch the War weapons: tanks, guns,
Dreaming blood and Death.

Harlem

Streetwalking woman,
Leaning in Harlem Hallway:
Sister of my soul!

FOR LANGSTON HUGHES

Gone   Gone
   Another weaver of black dreams has gone
we sat in June Bug's pad with the shades drawn
and the air thick with holy smoke. and we heard
the Lady sing Langston before we knew his name.
and when Black Bodies stopped swinging June
But, TG and I went out and swung on some white cats.
now I don't think the Mythmaker meant for us to do *that*
but we didn't know what else to do.

Gone   Gone
   Another weaver of black dreams has gone

WELCOME BACK, MR. KNIGHT:
LOVE OF MY LIFE

Welcome back, Mr. K: Love of My Life—
How's your drinking problem?—your thinking
Problem? you / are / pickling
Your liver—
Gotta / watch / out for the
"Ol Liver": Love of My Life.
How's your dope
Problem?—your marijuana, methadone, and cocaine
Problem / too?—your lustful problem—
How's your weight problem—your eating problem?
How's your lying and cheating and
Staying out all / night long problem?
Welcome back, Mr. K: Love of My Life
How's your pocket / book problem?—your / being
broke problem? you still owe and borrowing mo'
25 dollar problems from other / po / poets?
Welcome back, Mr. K: Love of My Life.
How's your ex-convict problem?—your John Birch
Problem?—your preacher problem?—your fat
Priests sitting in your / chair, saying
How racist and sexist they / will / forever / be
Problem?—How's your Daniel Moynihan
Problem?—your crime in the streets, runaway
Daddy, Black men with dark shades
And bulging crotches problem?
How's your nixon-agnew—j. edgar hoover
Problem?—you still paranoid? still schizoid?—
Still scared shitless?
How's your bullet-thru-the-brain problem?—or
A needle-in-your-arm problem?

Welcome back, Mr. K:—Love of My Life.
You gotta watch / out for the "Ol Liver."
How's your pussy
Problem?—lady-on-top—
smiling like God, titty-in-your-mouth
Problem? Welcome back, Mr. K:
Love of My Life. How's your peace
Problem?—your no / mo' war
Problem—your heart problem—your belly / problem?—
You gotta watch / out for the "Ol Liver."

ANOTHER POEM FOR ME
(after Recovering from an O.D.)

what now
what now dumb nigger damn near dead
what now
now that you won't dance
behind the pale white doors of death
what now   is   to be
to be what you wanna be
or what white / america wants you to be
a lame crawling from nickel bag to nickel bag
be black brother / man be black
and blooming in the night
be black like your fat brother
sweating and straining to hold you
as you struggle against the straps
be black   be black like
your woman   her painted face floating
above you   her hands sliding
                    under the sheets
to take yours   be black like
your mamma sitting in a quiet corner
praying to a white / jesus to save her black boy

what now dumb nigger damn near dead
where is the correctness
the proper posture
the serious love of living
now that death has fled these quiet corridors

THE BONES OF MY FATHER

1

There are no dry bones
here in this valley. The skull
of my father grins
at the Mississippi moon
from the bottom
of the Tallahatchie,
the bones of my father
are buried in the mud
of these creeks and brooks that twist
and flow their secrets to the sea.
but the wind sings to me
here the sun speaks to me
of the dry bones of my father.

2

There are no dry bones
in the northern valleys, in the Harlem alleys
young / black / men with knees bent
nod on the stoops of the tenements
and dream
of the dry bones of my father.

And young white longhairs who flee
their homes, and bend their minds
and sing their songs of brotherhood
and no more wars are searching for
my father's bones.

3

There are no dry bones here.
We hide from the sun.
No more do we take the long straight strides.
Our steps have been shaped by the cages
that kept us. We glide sideways
like crabs across the sand.
We perch on green lilies, we search
beneath white rocks . . .
THERE ARE NO DRY BONES HERE.

The skull of my father
grins at the Mississippi moon
from the bottom
of the Tallahatchie.

Connecticut
February 21, 1971

EVOLUTIONARY POEM NO. 1

I ain't got nobody
that I can depend on
                'cept myself

Etheridge Knight
New York City
August 1972

EVOLUTIONARY POEM NO. 2

We ain't got nobody
that we can depend on
                'cept ourselves.

Etheridge Knight
Memphis, Tennessee
September 1979

A POEM FOR MYSELF
(or Blues for a Mississippi Black Boy)

I was born in Mississippi;
I walked barefooted thru the mud.
Born black in Mississippi,
Walked barefooted thru the mud.
But, when I reached the age of twelve
I left that place for good.
Said my daddy chopped cotton
And he drank his liquor straight.
When I left that Sunday morning
He was leaning on the barnyard gate.
Left her standing in the yard
With the sun shining in her eyes.
And I headed North
As straight as the Wild Goose Flies,
I been to Detroit & Chicago
Been to New York city too.
I been to Detroit & Chicago
Been to New York city too.
Said I done strolled all those funky avenues
I'm still the same old black boy with the same old blues.
Going back to Mississippi
This time to stay for good
Going back to Mississippi
This time to stay for good—
Gonna be free in Mississippi
Or dead in the Mississippi mud.

45

REPORT TO THE MOTHER

Well, things / be / pretty bad now, Mother—
Got very little to eat.
The kids got no shoes for their tiny feet.
Been fighting with my woman, and one / other
Woe: —Ain't got a cent to pay the rent.

Been oiling / up / my pistol too—
Tho I / be / down with the flu,
So what / are / You going to do . . . ?

O Mother don't sing me
To the Father to fix / it—
He will blow-it. He fails
            and kills
His sons—and / *you* / know it.

THE SUN CAME

And if sun comes
How shall we greet him?
—Gwen Brooks

The sun came, Miss Brooks,—
After all the night years.
He came spitting fire from his lips.
And we flipped—We goofed the whole thing.
It looks like our ears were not equipped
For the fierce hammering.

And now the Sun has gone, has bled red,
Weeping behind the hills.
Again the night shadows form.
But beneath the placid face a storm rages.
The rays of Red have pierced the deep, have struck
The core. We cannot sleep.
The shadows sing: Malcolm, Malcolm, Malcolm.
The darkness ain't like before.

The Sun came, Miss Brooks.
And we goofed the whole thing.
I think.
(Though ain't no vision visited my cell.)

IT WAS A FUNKY DEAL

It was a funky deal.
The only thing real was red,
Red blood around his red, red beard.

It was a funky deal.

In the beginning was the word,
And in the end the deed.
Judas did it to Jesus
For the same Herd. Same reason.
You made them mad, Malcolm. Same reason.

It was a funky deal.

You rocked too many boats, man.
Pulled too many coats, man.
Saw through the jive.
You reached the wild guys
Like me. You and Bird. (And that
Lil LeRoi cat.)

It was a funky deal.

DARK PROPHECY: I SING OF SHINE

And, yeah, brothers
while white / america sings about the unsink-
able molly brown
(who was hustling the titanic
when it went down)
I sing to thee of Shine
the stoker who was hip enough to flee the fucking ship
and let the white folks drown
with screams on their lips
(jumped his black ass into the dark sea, Shine did,
broke free from the straining steel).
Yeah, I sing to thee of Shine
and how the millionaire banker stood on the deck
and pulled from his pockets a million dollar check
saying Shine Shine save poor me
and I'll give you all the money a black boy needs—
how Shine looked at the money and then at the sea
and said jump in mothafucka and swim like me—
And Shine swam on—Shine swam on—
and how the banker's daughter ran naked on the deck
with her pink tits trembling and her pants roun her neck
screaming Shine Shine save poor me
and I'll give you all the pussy a black boy needs—
how Shine said now pussy is good and that's no jive
but you got to swim not fuck to stay alive—
And Shine swam on Shine swam on—

How Shine swam past a preacher afloating on a board
crying save *me* nigger Shine in the name of the Lord—
and how the preacher grabbed Shine's arm and broke his stroke—
how Shine pulled his shank and cut the preacher's throat—
And Shine swam on—Shine swam on—
And when the news hit shore that the titanic had sunk
Shine was up in Harlem damn near drunk

49

FOR MALCOLM, A YEAR AFTER

Compose for Red a proper verse;
Adhere to foot and strict iamb;
Control the burst of angry words
Or they might boil and break the dam.
Or they might boil and overflow
And drench me, drown me, drive me mad.
So swear no oath, so shed no tear,
And sing no song blue Baptist sad.
Evoke no image, stir no flame,
And spin no yarn across the air.
Make empty anglo tea lace words—
Make them dead white and dry bone bare.

Compose a verse for Malcolm man,
And make it rime and make it prim.
The verse will die—as all men do—
But not the memory of him!
Death might come singing sweet like C,
Or knocking like the old folk say,
The moon and stars may pass away,
But not the anger of that day.

A POEM OF ATTRITION

I do not know if the color of the day
Was blue, pink, green, or August red.
I only know it was summer, a Thursday,
And the trestle above our heads
Sliced the sun into black and gold bars
That fell across our shiny backs
And shimmered like flat snakes on the water,
Worried by the swans, shrieks, jackknives,
And timid gainers—made bolder
As the day grew older.
Then Pooky Dee, naked chieftain, poised,
Feet gripping the black ribs of wood,
Knees bent, butt out, long arms
Looping the air, challenged
The great "two 'n' a half" gainer . . .
I have forgotten the sound of his capped
Skull as it struck the block . . .
The plop of a book dropped? The tear of a sheer blouse?
I do not know if the color of the day
Was blue, pink, green, or August red.
I only know the blood slithered, and
Our silence rolled like oil
Across the wide green water.

FOR BLACK POETS
WHO THINK OF SUICIDE

Black Poets should live—not leap
From steel bridges (like the white boys do).
Black Poets should live—not lay
Their necks on railroad tracks (like the white boys do).
Black Poets should seek—but not search too much
In sweet dark caves, nor hunt for snipe
Down psychic trails (like the white boys do).

For Black Poets belong to Black People. Are
The Flutes of Black Lovers. Are
The Organs of Black Sorrows. Are
The Trumpets of Black Warriors.
Let All Black Poets die as Trumpets,
And be buried in the dust of marching feet.

FOR MARY ELLEN McANALLY

Who is a white / woman / and
a perfect poem
and a song
pulse of love
world of wonders
and the warm black earth
falling thru my fingers

THE KEEPING OF A PROMISE

—for Charlene Blackburn

There / is / no moon tonight
No soft round globe to light

A golden path for me.
You have snatched our sun(s)
And flown outta sight. Like
A ship will sink
At the edge of the sea.

I / am / left alone to think,
And see Karl's football
Still rocking on the porch,
And Zack's diapers all
Funky with piss.

I feel and smell this—
Along with the talcum from your blouse
That you left in your sudden lurch
From this house.

ILU, THE TALKING DRUM

The deadness was threatening us—15 Nigerians and 1 Mississippi
    nigger.
It hung heavily, like stones around our necks, pulling us down
to the ground, black arms and legs outflung
on the wide green lawn of the big white house
The deadness was threatening us, the day
was dying with the sun, the stillness—
unlike the sweet silence after love / making or
the pulsating quietness of a summer night—
the stillness was skinny and brittle and wrinkled
by the precise people sitting on the wide white porch
of the big white house . . .
The darkness was threatening us, menacing . . .
we twisted, turned, shifted positions, picked our noses,
stared at our bare toes, hissed air thru our teeth . . .
Then Tunji, green robes flowing as he rose,
strapped on Ilu, the talking drum,
and began:

kah doom / kah doom-doom / kah doom / kah doom-doom-doom
kah doom / kah doom-doom / kah doom / kah doom-doom-doom
kah doom / kah doom-doom / kah doom / kah doom-doom-doom
kah doom / kah doom-doom / kah doom / kah doom-doom-doom

the heart, the heart beats, the heart, the heart beats slow
the heart beats slowly, the heart beats
the blood flows slowly, the blood flows
the blood, the blood flows, the blood, the blood flows slow
kah doom / kah doom-doom / kah doom / kah doom-doom-doom
and the day opened to the sound

kah doom / kah doom-doom / kah doom / kah doom-doom-doom
and our feet moved to the sound of life
kah doom / kah doom-doom / kah doom / kah doom-doom-doom
and we rode the rhythms as one
from Nigeria to Mississippi
and back
kah doom / kah doom-doom / kah doom / kah doom-doom-doom

POEM FOR THE LIBERATION
OF SOUTHERN AFRICA

have danced in ecstasy
(That's all—all I got
But for Love)
That leaps and sings across the sea
To the cell of *Nelson Mandela*
Sitting with his / own / self on Robbins Island
That precious prison of South Africa,
While Nelson Rockefeller is hailing fellows
for burying bones in the prison moonlight of Attica—
(That's all—all
but for Love)
And Time and drums
Beating Black feet beating
The dust. Dancing. Memories
Like fire. Dancing. Feet
Dangling from a lynching tree
In liberated Mississippi—
(That's all—all
But for Love)
And white mission / aries becoming "revolution / aries"
And hiding their crosses
Between their legs—
They huddle in circles then hurry away
To demon / strate
(And sing your wet eyes O Mother Africa.)
"Leaflet the banks."
"Down with the krugerrand."
"March on the embassies."
"No U.S. Troops in Africa."
"Give 'em some white / pussy—

That's all them Africans want, anyways . . ."
That's all—all
(But for Love)
And an ocean of us
Rising, reaching
Cause.—Cause? Yeah, Cause—'cause
I'm so busy
Pulling Charlie's foot outta / my / own / ass
And no job
And no land at / all
That's all.—All
I got—(But for Love.)

TELEVISION SPEAKS

Television speaks:
"Blacks die on Soweto Streets!"
On Cape Cod, indolents
Buy "burgers" and sticky sweets!

ON WATCHING POLITICIANS PERFORM
AT MARTIN LUTHER KING'S FUNERAL

Hypocrites shed tears
like shiny snake skins

words rolling
thru the southern air

the scent of flowers
mingles with Jack Daniels
and Cutty Sark

the last snake skin slithers
to the floor where
black baptist feet
have danced in ecstasy

they turn
away
to begin
again

manicured fingers shuffling
the same stacked deck
with the ante
raised

4

A FABLE

—for Etheridge Bombata and Mary Tandiwe

Once upon a today and yesterday and nevermore there were 7 men and women all locked / up in prison cells. Now these 7 men and women were innocent of any crimes; they were in prison because their skins were black. Day after day, the prisoners paced their cells, pining for their freedom. And the non-black jailers would laugh at the prisoners and beat them with sticks and throw their food on the floor. Finally, prisoner #1 said, "I will educate myself and emulate the non-colored people. That is the way to freedom— c'mon, you guys, and follow me." "Hell, no," said prisoner #2. "The *only* way to get free is to pray to my god and he will deliver you like he delivered Daniel from the lion's den, so unite and follow me." "Bullshit," said prisoner #3. "The *only* way / out is thru this tunnel i've been quietly digging, so c'mon, and follow me." "Uh-uh," said prisoner #4, "that's too risky. The only right / way is to follow all the rules and don't make the non-colored people angry, so c'mon brothers and sisters and unite behind me." "Fuck you!" said prisoner #5. "The *only* way / out is to shoot our way out, if all of you get / together behind me." "No," said prisoner #6, "all of you are incorrect; you have not analyzed the political situation by my scientific method and historical meemeejeebee. All we have to do is wait long enough and the bars will bend from their own inner rot. That is the *only* way." "All of you are crazy," cried prisoner #7. "I'll get out by myself, by ratting on the rest of you to the non-colored people. That is the way, that is the *only* way!" "No-no," they / all cried, "come and follow me. I have the / way, the only way to freedom." And so they argued, and to this day they are still arguing; and to this day they are still in their prison cells, their stomachs / trembling with fear.

MEMO #9

doze o blk / capitalists
ain't shit,
the blk / poet sung,
as he hustled his books
for 10.95.

MEMO #32

JOE WILLIAMS is
a very definite
Person,
Black / face
and all.

MEMO #2

The Blood stepped
Off the curb and waved
for a taxi; he was cleaner
Than a broke / dick dog.

MEMO #5

—for A. M. P.

I do crazy things when
I'm away from you: like
putting a match in my mouth
and striking the cigarette.

PORTRAIT OF MARY

my wife sleeps
her left arm outflung
toward the wall
her hair on the pillow sleeps too.
sometimes she snores
and I kick her on the leg
she moans and backs
her butt to me.
i go to sleep
my hand cupping her breast.

MY UNCLE IS MY HONOR
AND A GUEST IN MY HOUSE

—for Jim Cozart and Ezekiel Mphalele

1

In the center of the bloodvein
        is a kinkiss
        is a boiling
        and a calling
of your name
in the nighttime.

From the corners
of the curtained rooms
and down the bone-filled alleys
where the bible
        and the blade lay
like lovers
the shadows flee like common
thieves in the night
before the gold / bright teeth
of my Uncle
        Who is my Honor
and a Guest in my House.

2

The fakes, the unforgivers,
the fear-feeders, and the CIA
deny the kinkiss
and sing the silly song
        of "individualism" —
like gene autry riding / off / into the sunset
alone —

and point to the stones
falling from my tongue—
as I call out your name
                in the nighttime
from the cave
crossed with spears
on whose walls are written:
"All peoples shit over two shoes
and put on their pants one leg at a time."

3

In the center of the circle
stands my Uncle, legs apart
                singing poems
                to the short men
who squat in the shadows
and shake their fists
at the darkening sky.

I AND YOUR EYES

—for Mary McAnally

And I   and your eyes
Draw round about a ring of gold
And sing their circle of sparks
And I   and your eyes
Hold untold tales and conspire
With moon and sun to shake my soul.

And I   and your eyes
If I could hold your hillside smile
Your seashore laughter   your lips

Then I
Could stand alone   the pain
Of flesh   alone   the time and space
And steel   alone   but I am shaken
It has taken   your eyes
To move this stone.

ON THE BIRTH OF A BLACK / BABY / BOY

—for Isaac BuShie Blackburn-Knight

In Memphis—in Tennessee.
(O Come—and go / wid / meeee . . .)
In Memphis, in Tennessee—
In the year of (y) our Lord, 1978—
        (and the christian / suicides in Guyana).
In the bubbles and the blood of Boss Crump's guilt—
In the blueness of the hospitality of his / hos / pi / tal—
In the sterile gowns, green and growing—
In Memphis, in Tennessee . . .

Where all women / are / whining Queens,
Where black walnuts drop like leaves,
Where all women / are / shining Queens—
Where / cops / act / much worse than thieves—
In Memphis, in Tennessee . . .

When / the blood of your birth / is / screaming forth
        like a fountain
           from
        the white thighs of your mother—
When / her / hand / is tight on mine—
When I sink in / side her belly, and cling to / you—
When / short miles to the south the Ku Klux / Klan
        march like locusts over / this / land—
When mayors / like Moscone / are / shot-down, like
        Martin, Malcolm, and Medgar Evers—
When Jimmy Carter / tries / to *stand* where Martin *stood*
In Memphis, in Tennessee—And.

As the lady / medic / with her long black hair
        taunts your mother: O push push push *push*—

As / my / belly / becomes a drum and my blood beseech thee —
As / my / heart / becomes a song and my eyes lakes of lightning.
As / your / mother grunts for 3 / days and groans for 3 / nights,
As / she issues you / forth on a sunday night,
               (on a chilling, raining, sun / day / night) —
               and now.
As you lay warming in my arms, son —
               all I / can / say is:
You / be a loonngg time coming, boy —
But you're wel / come here.

November–December 1978

BIRTHDAY POEM

The sun rose today, and
The sun went down
Over the trees beyond the river;
No crashing thunder
Nor jagged lightning
Flashed my forty-four years across
The heavens. I am here.
I am alone. With the Indianapolis / News

Sitting, under this indiana sky
I lean against a gravestone and feel
The warm wine on my tongue.
My eyes move along the corridors
Of the stars, searching
For a sign, for a certainty

As definite as the cold concrete
Pressing against my back.
Still the stars mock
Me and the moon is my judge.

But only the moon.

'Cause I ain't screwed no thumbs
Nor dropped no bombs—
Tho my name is naughty to the ears of some
And I ain't revealed the secrets of my brothers
Tho my balls've / been pinched
And my back's / been / scarred—

And I ain't never stopped loving no / one
O I never stopped loving no / one

Indianapolis, Indiana
April 19, 1975

COP-OUT SESSION

I done shot dope, been to jail, swilled
wine, ripped off sisters, passed bad checks,
changed my name, howled at the moon,
wrote poems, turned
backover flips, flipped over backwards
(in other words)
I been confused, fucked up, scared, phony
and jive
to a whole / lot of people . . .

Haven't you?

       In one way or another?

Enybody else wanna cop-out?

A POEM TO GALWAY KINNELL

Saturday, April 26, 1973
Jefferson, Missouri 65101
(500 yards, as the crow flies,
from where I am writing you
this letter, lies the Missouri
State Prison—it lies, the prison,
like an overfed bear alongside
the raging missouri river—
the pale prison, out of which
sonny liston, with clenched fist,
fought his way, out of which,
james earl ray ripped his way
into the hearts of us all . . .)

dear galway,
 it is flooding here, in missouri,
the lowlands are all under water and at night
the lights dance on the dark water,
our president, of late of watergate,
is spozed to fly above the flooded areas
and estimate how much damage has been done
to THE PEOPLES . . .

dear galway,
 it is lonely here, and sometimes,
THE PEOPLES can be a bitch

dear galway,
 i hear poems in my head
as the wind blows in your hair

and the young brown girl
with the toothpaste smile
who flows freely because she has heard OUR SOUNDS . . .

dear galway,
        OUR SONGS OF LOVE are still
murmurs among these melodies of madness . . .
dear galway, and what the fuck are the irish doing /
and when the IRA sends JUST ONE, just one soldier
to fight with say the American Indians, then i'll believe them . . .

dear galway,
        the river is rising here, and i am
scared and lonely . . .

Mary and the children send their love
to you and yours

                always

                Etheridge Knight

MISSOURI HAIKU

Boone County

A blue pick / up truck
Roars past; Sun shines on shotgun
Leering in window

Outside St. Louis

Route 66 curves
West—an arrow piercing the
Bleeding eye of God

Clay County

Thunder in the hills
And caves; goldenrods mourn war
Echoes of "Frank'n'Jess."

Mizzu

ROTC March:
Drums roll and die. White blossoms
Float in Summer air.

INDIANA HAIKU

Riverside Park

A brown oak tree leans
In the arms of his brother:
Squir'lls leap, limb to limb.

Indiana Avenue, 1949

Neons flash red and green.
April rains on still street, Man
Nods, Red lights blink, blink.

Mirror of keen blades
Slender as guitar strings; Wes
Montgomery jazz.

Indianapolis Winter, 1973

Icicles crack and drop
In the crusty snow; skaters
Glide on frozen pond.

WE FREE SINGERS BE

*"If we didn't have music, dancers would / be soldiers too,
holding guns in their arms, instead of each / other."*
—Father Boniface Hardin

We free singers be
sometimes swimming in the music,
like porpoises playing in the sea.
We free singers be
come agitators at times, be
come eagles circling the sun,
hurling stones at hunters, be
come scavengers cracking eggs
in the palm of our hands.
(Remember, oh, do you remember
the days of the raging fires
when I clenched my teeth
in my sleep and refused to speak
in the daylight hours?)
We free singers be, baby
tall walkers, high steppers,
hip shakers, we free singers be
still waters sometimes too.
(Remember, oh, do you remember
the days when children held our hands
and danced
around us in circles, and we laughed in the sun?)
(Remember, oh, do you remember
how we slept in the shade of the trees
and woke, trembling in the darkness?)
We free singers be
voyagers
and sing of cities with straight streets
and mountains piercing the moon—
and rivers that never run dry.

(Remember, oh, do you remember
the snow
falling
on broadway
and the soldiers marching
thru the icy streets
with blood on their coat sleeves?)
(Remember, oh, do you remember
how we left the warm movie house
turned up our collars
and rode the subway home?)
We free singers be, baby.
We free singers be.

TALKING IN THE WOODS
WITH KARL AMORELLI

The old Toyota, green as a frog, coughs and clanks,
Shoots its last wad, throws its last rod,
Sighs and dies, bumps and hops to a stop on the Interstate—
Twenty miles from Worcester, the neat New England
City of three deck flats. Here my lover lives
And sets her plate, and lies late with me in the mornings.
The ride from Boston had / been / a merry-go-round of touching
And talking and wide-eyed smiles and body smells.
Now, like hail striking a tin roof, gravel pelts the fenders.
We get out and look around. There is a lake to our right
Surrounded by green: cedars, oaks, willows, ferns and lilies.
After consultations and imaginations, we decide
That she / could / catch a ride much better than I—
Being blond, blue-eyed, and a woman on the side.
"Well, catch a trucker then," I smarted, and turned
To Karl, this brown-eyed boy
With curly hair, this love / child of the woman
I love. "C'mon, Karl," I say,
"Let's check / out / the lake on this bright and good day."
We scramble over the fence and walk into the woods.
The beer bears on my bladder. We wander through the trees.
"I gotta pee," I say,—"what about you?"
"Me too."
Legs apart, urine splattering the dry leaves—
Me looking at the lake—
He looking at me.
"I can pee further than you, Eth."
"Yeah, I see."
"And *higher,* too."
"Yeah, Karl, the older you are—

The lower your arc."
"You mean, like flat feet?"
"No—like this." I make the motion with my hand,
And say, "Like a rainbow, boy."
"Well? why?—well? *why?*"
We dance, prance (the last few drops go down our pants),
Shake and zip.
"Well, dude," I say, "it's like this—speaking
from a psychological, physiological, chronological, and—
Sexiological standpoint of view . . ."
"*Eth* / ridge!"
I laugh. He laughs.
We crash outta the woods, tumble / over / the fence
And face our Lover.
Sunlight glints / off / her glasses.
"What were you / two / *doing* so long?"
"Well," I said,
"Karl was pissing—
Me?—I / was / peeing."

BOSTON 5:00 A.M.—10/74

AWAKE! For mornings
Are the same as nights
The troops
Goosestep
Down the streets

A POEM ON THE MIDDLE EAST "PEACE PROCESS"

Israel à la Begin, begins: "We
/ love / peace-and-ah
Yakady-yakady-yak-yak-yak.
That's why we / drove /
the Palestinians off / their / land—
With the help of america and england's evil hand.
And-ah-yakady-yakady-yak-yak-yak."

In the Gaza strip an Arab boy sleeps,
his knees / are / drawn / up to his chest.
His hands cup his crotch. He dreams of grenades,
And machine guns and prayers to Allah.

An Israeli boy sleeps in Tel Aviv. He dreams
Of the tales told to him by his / grand / father:
Nazi boots goosestepping on cobblestone, of lampshades
Made / from Jewish skin, of Jewish women—and men—
Naked and torn. He dreams too of blooming gardens
In the "promised land" and of killing Arabs
At his Rabbi's command.

And the *Peacemakers?*" Ah, the peacemakers
Give guns to / one
And bombs to the / other
All contrary to the / cries / of the Mother.

HAIKU 1

A slender finger of light
pokes a golden finger
in the bare black stage.

MEMO #43

You get the blues in twos
When you / be living
Like I / be living
In Memphis Tennessee

1979

AND TELL ME POET,
CAN LOVE EXIST IN SLAVERY?

Come then Poet, and sing
To me a TRUE SONG
Of white doves circling the horizon—
Of Guitars strumming the evening calm.

Can we forget, poet,
The right and wrong
Done, the gushing blood,
The broken bone
Shattering the moon-night,
The exiled son,
The fugitive daughter?

O Poet, your tongue
is split, and as still
as the Stone
In the Belly of the Great Mother.
She has always known:
Love and Freedom are One!

(All the rest is, at best—
A melted ice cream cone.)

GREEN GRASS AND YELLOW BALLOONS

—for Alexandria Keller, a poet at four

the garden we walked in
was dead / dying
and the fine / rain fell
you held / my hand
fine / rain falling
cold wind blowing
rain thru your hair
dead world dying
re / born
by your words
warm and soft and brown
like your eyes
etheridge, you said, i've
composed a poem for you

green grass
and yellow balloons
floating in the sky
you sang of. and sadness too.
softly you sang
your words warming me
and the sea rose in me
and your song sent me spinning
and i thought of e e cummings
mud puddles and colored marbles
and what the fuck was i doing
in this new / england / state—
then your eyes seemed sadder to me
and your words seemed warmer to me
and the sea rose higher in me
and suddenly
i was 4 and you were 40

and we were one
as the fine / rain fell
harder
and harder
and harder
till we came to the white / fence
that separated
US
from the River
so soon so soon
do yellow balloons
burst
demons stalk / this land
that smash
people and poets
whether 4 or 40
so soon so soon
will your words
be eagles
that rise screaming
from the warmth of their nest
to soar
above this freeze
and froze and frigid land
and we
who walk in new ways
will hear you
we will hear you—
and sing too
of green grass. and yellow balloons

Waterford, Connecticut
October 21, 1971

BELLY SONG

—for the Daytop Family

"You have made something
Out of the sea that blew
And rolled you on its salt bitter lips.
It nearly swallowed you.
But I hear
You are tough and harder to swallow than most . . ."
                                    —S. Mansfield

1

And I   and I / must admit
that the sea in you
        has sung / to the sea / in me
and I   and I / must admit
that the sea in me
        has fallen / in love
        with the sea in you
because you have made something
out of the sea
        that nearly swallowed you

And this poem
This poem
This poem / I give / to you.
This poem is a song / I sing / I sing / to you
from the bottom
        of the sea
                in my belly

This poem / is a song / about FEELINGS
about the Bone of feeling
about the Stone of feeling
        And the Feather of feeling

2

This poem
This poem
This poem / is /
a death / chant
and a grave / stone
and a prayer for the dead:
    for young Jackie Robinson.
a moving Blk / warrior who walked
among us
    with a wide / stride—and heavy heels
moving   moving   moving
thru the blood and mud and shit of Vietnam
moving   moving   moving
thru the blood and mud and dope of America
    for Jackie / who was /

a song
and a stone
and a Feather of feeling
    now dead
and / gone / in this month of love

This poem
This poem / is / a silver feather
and the sun-gold / glinting / green hills breathing
river flowing . . .

3

This poem
This poem
This poem / is / for ME—for me
and the days / that lay / in the back / of my mind

when the sea / rose up /
        to swallow me
and the streets I walked
        were lonely streets
        were stone / cold streets

This poem
This poem / is /
for me / and the nights
        when I
wrapped my feelings
        in a sheet of ice
and stared
        at the stars
            thru iron bars
            and cried
in the middle of my eyes . . .

This poem
This poem
This poem / is / for me
        and my woman
        and the yesterdays
when she opened
        to me like a flower
        But I fell on her
        like a stone
I fell on her like a stone . . .

4
And now—in my 40th year
        I have come here
to this House of Feelings
to this Singing Sea

and I   and I / must admit
that the sea in me
      has fallen / in love
with the sea in you
because the sea
that now sings / in you
      is the same sea
that nearly swallowed you—
      and me too.

Seymour, Connecticut
June 1971

APOLOGY FOR APOSTASY?

Soft songs, like birds, die in poison air
So my song cannot now be candy.
Anger rots the oak and elm; roses are rare,
Seldom seen through blind despair.

And my murmur cannot be heard
Above the din and damn. The night is full
Of buggers and bastards; no moon or stars
Light the sky. And my candy is deferred

Till peacetime, when my voice shall be light,
Like down, lilting in the air; then shall I
Sing of beaches, white in the magic sun,
And of moons and maidens at midnight.

CON/TIN/U/WAY/SHUN BLUES

Well, the las' time I saw my mother
She said, son, take care of yourself—
'Cause when it gets / down to the nitty gritty
Boy, you ain't got nobody else.

                    ain't nobody else
                    ain't nobody else

You talk about my friends, baby
                you say
Ain't none of them niggas no good
What about my white friends, baby,
Do they do the things they should
                even if they could—
                even if they could

      "blues are more than cries of oppression"
          —Mary Helen Washington

They say the blues is just a slave song
But I say that's just a lie
Cause even when we be free, baby—
Lord knows we still have got to die
                lovers will still lie
                babies will still cry

Some folks don't like my way of living
Some folks, oh, they don't like my life
Well, some folks don't like my mama—
And some, oh, they don't like my wife

Yeah, the man done lost his niggas
And he done blowed his children too
Now he's 'bout to lose his woman—
And he don't know what to do

                    he still got guns, honey
                    and a whole lotta money

Well, I know a girl named Wanda
Yeah, and she flat backs all night long
Yeah, she be staring at the ceiling
While the truckers hump and moan

                    so drunk from gin
                    that she's gotta put it in

Sometimes, I think, lady,
That our troubles will never end
But when I wake up in the morning—
I start out all over again

'Cause I gotta keep on pushing
I gotta keep on keeping on
I know one day we'll be free, baby,
And most troubles will be gone.

5

ON SEEING THE BLACK MALE
AS #1 SEX OBJECT IN AMERICA

There / are / Black men in the south
Of America who / are soooooooo pretty
That their beauty
Sucks in fat gulps the breath from your mouth.
In Nashville, Memphis, Jackson, Lil Rock,
In spots that / are / just dots
On the hi / way to the south and sun—
Tall, "male" men—
Wearing flashing red caps, and hats
With wide brims in bold green, grin.
Black men in the south
Of America / are / soooooooo pretty—
In bright jeans, in tight jeans, bulging;
Shining their cars,
Hanging in the bars,
Leaning on the corners
Where the snow / janes pass
Stroking the Black male asses
From behind dark glasses,—
Where the crow / janes pass—and wonder too
And stroke too and gulp too and know too—
That it / is / true:
Black men in the south
Of America / are / soooooooo pretty
That men, and women, hide
Under sheets and masks and ride
And plot under the Alabama moon
How to "cut the nut."

LAST WORDS BY "SLICK"
(or a self / sung eulogy)

Now, when I / die, dont you bury me
On no lone prairie;
And dont put me in no plain pine box
(cause I left plenty cold cash!);
And throw my cold butt in the deep blue sea.
Whatever you do, dont plant me / in no six feet of dirt;
Just mash me, mash me, except for my dick,
Which I want wrapped in a white / woman's skirt.

I dont want no preacher / man a-preaching
Over me—cause I know where I am going.
I dont want no tears, no flowers,
No standing around and waiting / up / all hours.
Just get a golden trumpet, and have Dizzy blow it.
Cause I / wuz / Slick—and you damn well know it.

No piano playing, no blues *please;*
No moaning and groaning;
Just lay me on the table, mash me
Into my two-hundred-dollar suit,
Red socks, black patent leather shoes,
Polka-dot tie (make damn shore it's silk—
And dont forget it!)

Take me out to my pink cadillac
Prop me up / under the steering wheel,
Tow me out to real high hill,
Dig a hole—twenty feet long and twenty feet wide,
Place a giant joint of reefer / weed by my side;
Then leave me *alone*—
And let me drive to hell in style!

HAIKU

Two hours I've walked . . .
. . . this Tulsa rain . . .
In her house, my wife sleeps, snoring.

Yellow Moon rise . . . hounds
Howl . . . my daughter weds soon.
O my heart is hollow?

Nurse hovers . . . belly
Aches . . . old wine, old bones . . .
O my sons! don't forget me

O Manhattan town!
Subways swallow / up Sonia—
My "highs" drove her / down!

O swaying trees,
Shining, dripping leaves . . .
Life's got me on my knees.

The Sun comes, the pain flees. . . .
Today I'll boogie down Broadway.
O come!—dance with me!

I'm shower'd . . . shaved . . .
Waiting on wooden bench . . .
Carol Ann visits today!

Open! O my heart's
Flower: Elizabetheridge!
I, springtime shower!

Some days slip by
            like clouds in the sky,
Or the glimpse of a girl
From the edge of the eye.

Gulls scream: "Breakfast!"
Waves lap against fishing boats.
In Puget I am cold.

Poor Martin L. King!
Death rains steel / down Beale Street
Poor Memphis Tennessee!

Woe South Africa!
Bullets, bones, fires of *Apartheid!*
My bowels won't move.

Sigh, cry, broken-hearted
Woman, alone . . . he smiled . . .
—Stole your welfare check!

Deta! O Deta!
Where are you? your guitar?
Your songs? your legs?—your *love?*

The beach, your bra falling . . .
Your cat dying . . . tears . . .
We climb the sand dunes.

Ah, Marisella!
This attic, this music,
Our motions, our tongues—aiiee!

Worcester woman,
Fair face of flat "A's,"
My belly / sing / son / soft, Memphis days!

The WORD, Was, Is, Will, BE:
The Beginning and the End, BE;
And the Word / is / Round
And Warm and Rolling;
A the Word / be / a Verb,
And the Verb / be / a Woman . . .

EAT
HELEN B HAPPY
(a found poem)

Eat, Helen,
Be happy!

Eat, Helen,
Be happy!

"Eat it here?—
Or take it home?"

Be happy!
Helen be.

VARIOUS PROTESTATIONS
FROM VARIOUS PEOPLE

Esther say I drink too much.
Mama say pray dont think too much.
My shrink he say I feel too much,
And the cops say I steal too much;
Social Workers say I miss my Daddy too much,
That I dream of driving a Caddy too much.
White folks say I'm lazy and late too much,
Not objective—depend on fate too much.
Philosophers say I wanna BE too much.
Reagan say I talk about me too much,
Singing songs 'bout being free too much.

I say—sing about me being *free* too much?
Say sing about me being *free* too much?

AT A VA HOSPITAL IN THE MIDDLE
OF THE UNITED STATES OF AMERICA:
AN ACT IN A PLAY

Stars from five wars, scars,
Words filled with ice and fear,
Nightflares and fogginess,
and a studied regularity.
    Gon' lay down my sword 'n' shield—
    Down by the river side, down by the river side—
    Down by the river side . . .

Former Sergeant Crothers, among the worst,
Fought the first. He hears well, tho
He mumbles in his oatmeal. He
Was gassed outside Nice. We
Tease him about *"le pom-pom,"* and chant:
"There's a place in France where the women wear no pants."
Former Sergeant Crothers has gray whiskers
And a gracious grin,
But his eyes do not belie
His chemical high.
    Gon' lay down my sword 'n' shield—
    Down by the river side, down by the river side—
    Down by the river side . . .

A. C. Williams drove a half-track
"Half da goddamn way 'cross Africa
In da second war," his black
Face proclaims, and exclaims—
Along with other rosy exaggerations.
Each week he sneaks through the iron-wrought fence
To the Blinking Bar down the street.
Midnight reeks the red-eyes, the tired
Temper, the pains in the head.
A phone call summons an aide to bring A. C. to bed.

Ain't gon' study the war no more . . . Well,
I ain't gonna study the war no more—
Ain't gonna study the war no more—
O I ain't gonna study the war no more.

"Doc" Kramer, ex-medic in Korea
Is armless. And legless,
is an amazement of machines
And bubbling bottles. His nurse,
White starched and erect, beams
A calloused cheerfulness:
"How *are* we today?" Kramer's wife leans
Forward, sparkling fingers caressing his stump
Of arm. She is pink, fifty-six, and plump.
"Doc" Kramer desires sleep.

> *Gon' put on my long, white robe—*
> *Down by the river side, down by the river side—*
> *Down by the river side . . .*

Ex PFC Leonard Davenport goes to court
Tomorrow. He is accused of "possession and sale"
Of narcotics; his conditional bail
Was that he stay at the VA, for the cure.
For an end to sin,
For a surcease of sorrow.
He spends his pension for ten grams of "pure."
He nods the days away,
And curses his Ranger Colonel in fluent Vietnamese.
His tour in "Nam" is his golden prize.

> *Gon' put on my long, white robe—*
> *Down by the river side, down by the river side—*
> *Down by the river side . . .*

106

Grant Trotter's war was the south side
Of San Diego. Storming the pastel sheets
Of Mama Maria's, he got hit with a fifty
Dollar dose of syphilis. His feats
Are legends of masturbation, the constant coming
As he wanders the back streets of his mind.
The doctors whisper and huddle in fours
When Trotter's howls roam the corridors.
We listen. We are patient patients.

> *Ain't gon' study the war no more . . . Well,*
> *I ain't gonna study the war no more—*
> *Ain't gonna study the war no more—*
> *O I ain't gonna study the war no more.*

Indianapolis
September 1982

ON THE PROJECTS PLAYGROUND

Say, Mister!
Uh-huh?
You a poet / man?
Uh-huh, uh-huh.
Me too.
Uh-huh, uh-huh!

CIRCLING THE DAUGHTER

—for Tandi

You came / to be / in the Month of Malcolm,
And the rain fell with a fierce gentleness,
Like a martyr's tears,
On the streets of Manhattan when your light was lit;
And the City sang you Welcome. Now I sit,
Trembling in your presence. Fourteen years
Have brought the moon-blood, the roundness,
The girl-giggles, the grand-leaps.
We are touch-tender in our fears.

You break my eyes with your beauty:
Ooouu-oo-baby-I-love-you.

Do not listen to the lies of old men
Who fear your power,
Who preach that you were "born in sin."
A flower is moral by its own flowering.
Reach always within
For the Music and the Dance and the Circling.

O Tandiwe, by Beloved of this land,
Your spring will come early and
When the earth begins its humming,
Begin your dance with men
With a Grin and a Grace of whirling.
Your place is neither ahead nor behind,
Neither right nor left. The world is round.
Make the sound of your breathing
A silver bell at midnight
And the chilling wet of the morning dew . . .

You break my eyes with your beauty:
Ooouu-oo-baby-I-love-you.

109

FOR A BROOKLINE LADY I LOVE

So / zoom / your Special Spot
On / to Golden Greece—
Drink wine, dance—find release
From the Tight. (But do not
Forget *me*, please.)
And when the warm blanket of night
Covers the Sun, sleeping in Helen's sea,
Then rise with the Moon, I say
Rise with the Moon and fly to me
On silver wings, on silver wings; I pray
Your heart / be-all / in one piece.

ONCE ON A NIGHT IN THE DELTA:
A REPORT FROM HELL

—for Sterling Brown

Gravel rattles against the fenders of the van
The River flashes in the distance.
The wind is thick with the scent of honeysuckle.
The road from Greenville curves like the sickle
Of the new moon, now hanging over east Texas.
Moun' Bayou sleeps on a straight street.

The poor live on both / sides / of the tracks
In this town peopled by Blacks.
Tho the bloods / now / pack pistols
And rap on two-way radios,
And the homes of a few are spacious and new,
With sunken patios;
Tho the dice are / shot / thru a leather horn and
The whiskey burns my belly in the early morning,

We still shuffle in lines, like coffles of slaves:
Stamps for food—the welfare rolls and the voting polls.
We frown. Our eyes are dark caves

Of mourning.—So I'd like to report to you, Sir Brown—
Fromaway / down / here—
Mississippi is *still* hell, Sir Brown—
For me and ol Slim Greer.

June 1981

A BLACK POET LEAPS TO HIS DEATH

—for mbembe milton smith

was it a blast to the balls dear brother
with the wind ringing in the ear
that great rush against the air
that great push
                    into the universe

' you are not now alone mbembe
of the innocent eyes   sadder
than a mondays rain   it is i
who hear your crush of bone
                your splatter of brain
                your tear of flesh
on the cold chicago stone

                and my october cry
when the yellow moon is ringed with blood
of children dead in the lebanese mud
        is as sharp as a kc switchblade
your pain is a slash across my throat
i feel a chill   can the poet belie
the poem
        old revolutionaries never die
it is said
        they just be born again
(check chuck colson and his panther from folsom)
but you are *dead*
mbembe   poetman in the home of the brave
the brown leaves whister across you grave

but it must have been a rush   a great gasp
                    of breath
                    the awesome leap to your death
o poet of the blood and bone
                    of the short song
                    and serious belief
i sing you release

                                                                October 1981

                                    113

REHABILITATION & TREATMENT
IN THE PRISONS OF AMERICA

The Convict strolled into the prison administration building to get assistance and counseling for his personal problems. Inside the main door were several other doors proclaiming: Doctor, Lawyer, Teacher, Counselor, Therapist, etc. He chose the proper door, and was confronted with two more doors: Custody and Treatment. He chose Treatment, went in, and was confronted with two more doors: First Offender and Previous Offender. Again he chose the proper door and was confronted with two *more* doors: Adult and Juvenile. He was an adult, so he walked through that door and ran smack into two *more* doors: Democrat and Republican. He was democrat, so he rushed through that door and ran smack into two *more* doors: Black and White. He was Black, so he rushed— *ran*—through that door—and fell nine stories to the street.

ABOUT THE AUTHOR

Born in rural Mississippi in 1931, Etheridge Knight received little formal education. He served as an army-trained medical technician during the Korean War and was badly wounded. Later convicted of armed robbery, he spent six years in prison. "I died in Korea from a shrapnel wound," he wrote, "and narcotics resurrected me. I died in 1960 from a prison sentence and poetry brought me back to life."

Since his first book, *Poems from Prison*, appeared in 1968, Knight's poetry has been widely acclaimed. He was awarded fellowships by the Guggenheim Foundation and the National Endowment for the Arts, and in 1985 received the Shelley Memorial Award from the Poetry Society of America in recognition of distinguished achievement in poetry. Etheridge Knight died on March 10, 1991, at his home in Indianapolis, Indiana.